PIANO ACCOMPANIMENTS & ENSEMBLE SCORES

TEAM WOODWIND

CORMAC LOANE and RICHARD DUCKETT

International Music Publications

Edited by BARRIE CARSON TURNER

Piano accompaniments by GEOFFRY RUSSELL-SMITH and BARRIE CARSON TURNER

INTERNATIONAL MUSIC PUBLICATIONS would like to thank the following publishers for permission to use arrangements of their copyright material in TEAM WOODWIND.
IN THE MOOD - Words by JOE GARLAND, Music by ANDY RAZAF
© 1939 & 1991 Shapiro Bernstein & Co. Inc., USA
Sub-published by Peter Maurice Music Co. Ltd., London WC2H 0EA
I COULD HAVE DANCED ALL NIGHT - Words by ALAN JAY LERNER, Music by FREDERICK LOEWE
© 1956 & 1991 Alan Jay Lerner and Frederick Loewe
Chappell & Co. Inc., New York, NY, publisher and owner of allied rights throughout the world.
By arrangement with Lowal Corporation. Chappell Music Ltd., London W1Y 3FA
DON'T SIT UNDER THE APPLE TREE (WITH ANYONE ELSE BUT ME) - Words and Music by LEW BROWN, CHARLIE TOBIAS and SAM H. STEPT
© 1942 & 1991 Robbins Music Corporation USA
Redwood Music Ltd., London NW1 8BD/Memory Lane Music Ltd., London WC2H 8NA/EMI United Partnership Ltd., London WC2H 0EA
STRANGER ON THE SHORE - Words by ROBERT MELLIN, Music by ACKER BILK
© 1962 & 1991 EMI Music Publishing Ltd, London WC2H 0EA
MOONLIGHT SERENADE - Words by MITCHELL PARISH, Music by GLENN MILLER
© 1939 & 1991 Robbins Music Corporation, USA
EMI United Partnership Ltd., London WC2H 0EA
MOOD INDIGO - Words and Music by DUKE ELLINGTON, IRVING MILLS and ALBANY BIGARD
© 1931 & 1991 Gotham Music Service Inc, USA
Sub-published by EMI Music Publishing Ltd., London WC2H 0EA
WHAT A WONDERFUL WORLD - Words and Music by GEORGE DAVID WEISS & BOB THIELE
© 1967 & 1991 Herald Square Music Company, USA
Carlin Music Corp., London NW1 8BD
WATERMELON MAN - Music by HERBIE HANCOCK, Words by JIMI HENDRIX
© 1962 & 1991 Hancock Music Co.
B. Feldman & Co. Ltd., London WC2H 0EA
BLOWIN' IN THE WIND - Words and Music by BOB DYLAN
© 1963 & 1991 Witmark & Sons, USA
Warner Chappell Music Ltd., London W1Y 3FA
EDELWEISS (From THE SOUND OF MUSIC) - Lyrics by OSCAR HAMMERSTEIN II, Music by RICHARD RODGERS
Copyright © 1959 by Richard Rodgers and Oscar Hammerstein II
Copyright Renewed.
This arrangement Copyright © 1991 by WILLIAMSON MUSIC CO.
WILLIAMSON MUSIC owner of publication and allied rights throughout the world.
International Copyright Secured   All Rights Reserved
LOVE ME TENDER - Words and Music by VERA MATSON & ELVIS PRESLEY
© 1956 & 1991 Elvis Presley Music Inc., USA
Carlin Music Corp., London NW1 8BD
LITTLE DONKEY - Words and Music by ERIC BOSWELL
© 1959 & 1991 Chappell Music Ltd., London W1Y 3FA
THE PINK PANTHER - by HENRY MANCINI
© 1963 & 1991 United Artists Music Co. Inc., USA
EMI United Partnership Ltd., London WC2H 0EA
OVER THE RAINBOW - Words by E. Y. HARBURG, Music by HAROLD ARLEN
© 1938 & 1991 Leo Feist Inc., USA
EMI United Partnership Ltd., London WC2H 0EA
SWEET GEORGIA BROWN - Words and Music by BEN BERNIE, KENNETH CASEY & MACEO PINKARD
© 1925 & 1991 Remick Music Corp, USA
Sub-published by Francis Day & Hunter Ltd., London WC2H 0EA and Redwood Music Ltd., London NW1 8BD
STAR WARS Main Title - by JOHN WILLIAMS
© 1977 & 1991 Fox Fanfare Music Inc.
Warner Chappell Music Ltd., London W1Y 3FA

Sincere thanks are extended to the following people whose criticism, advice and help in various ways has been invaluable.
KEITH ALLEN, Head of Music Services for the City of Birmingham Education Department.
PHILIP BROOKES, Bassoonist.
PETER BULLOCK, Clarinet Teacher, Derbyshire County Education Department.
RICHARD REAKES, Oboe Teacher, City of Birmingham Education Department.
DAVID ROBINSON, Woodwind Teacher, Kirklees Education Department.
DEBRA SANDHAM, Oboe Teacher, St. Chad's, Lichfield Cathedral School.
JULIE SCHRODER, Flute Teacher, City of Birmingham Education Department.
ALISON WHATLEY, Oboe Teacher, City of Birmingham Education Department.
And also to the many pupils who have worked with the TEAM WOODWIND books in transcript form.
First Published 1991
© Copyright International Music Publications

Exclusive Distributors
International Music Publications, Southend Road, Woodford Green, Essex IG8 8HN, England.

Cover Design: Ian Barrett / David Croft
Cover Photography: Ron Goldby
Production: Stephen Clark / David Croft
Reprographics: Cloverleaf
Instruments photographed by courtesy of Vincent Bach International Ltd., London.
Typeset by Cromwell Typesetting & Design Ltd., London / Printed in England

TEAM WOODWIND:Piano Accompaniments / Ensemble Scores
ISBN 0 86359 786 6 /Order Ref:17536 / 215-2-657

Introducing Team Woodwind

The Individual Course

TEAM WOODWIND is structured to suit the requirements of all beginners, whatever their age or experience. New concepts are introduced singly and these are reinforced by Rhythm Grids for those who need them. As a general rule, the music at the top of each new 'concept page' is simpler than the music lower down the page and is particularly suitable for designing 'easy' courses for the youngest players. Courses which give more rapid progress can also be selected. For example, by proceeding via pages 2,3,4,5,7, and 15 and on to 18, the most able beginner can be playing an extended, fifty-bar accompanied solo - *Sleigh Ride* - within a few lessons.

Teachers of oboe, flute and saxophone who may like their pupils to explore more fully the low register in the early stages of playing, before moving on to the upper register will find appropriate supplementary material in TEAM WOODWIND for Clarinet on pages 4,5,6,7,8,9,14,16,17 and so on.

The ensemble material also provides music of varying complexity within the same playing range. So while children of primary school age will cope easily with *German Tune* and *Lullaby* on page 14, for example, the *Canzonetta* on page 15 will appeal particularly to secondary age pupils. Study options are provided at the foot of most pages so that the material can be used with great flexibility; the number of routes through TEAM WOODWIND is almost unlimited.

The Ensemble Course

TEAM WOODWIND ensemble music is drawn from Baroque, Classical and Folk Music, Hymns and Popular Songs and has been arranged so that it is playable by most combinations of instruments.

While the extended ensemble material starts on page 14, many of the pieces from pages 2 to 11 can be played together by certain instruments. Many of the tutorial pieces in the early part of the flute and oboe book are the same, for example, and the flute supplement carries many of the clarinet pieces transposed for unison performance.

All TEAM WOODWIND ensemble pieces are carefully graded. A group of beginners can therefore learn to play exclusively from this material, should the need arise. Or lessons can be timetabled so that pupils meet as a group every second or third week, perhaps alternating with individual or smaller group lessons. Some of the ensemble pieces are songs which will be well known to many children. This allows for a group of woodwind players to be integrated into a classroom music session, which might also include some percussion/keyboard accompaniment, as well as voices.

All B flat (clarinet) ensemble material in TEAM WOODWIND integrates fully with all ensemble material in TEAM BRASS. These arrangements can therefore be used for any combination of wind and brass players from duet right up to full symphonic wind band. Here are examples of some possible small combinations:

Oboe	Trumpet	Flute
Trumpet	Clarinet	Trumpet
B♭ Saxophone	E♭ Horn	Clarinet
	Bassoon	F Horn
		Bassoon

The combinations that can be derived from using TEAM WOODWIND and TEAM BRASS together are virtually limitless.

Listening Skills

In order to develop aural awareness from the early stages of learning, PLAY BY EAR lines have been included in each book. These offer the opportunity for pupils to play familiar tunes without musical notation.

A course on improvisation runs through the Saxophone book. This begins with a selection of LISTENING GAMES which gradually develop into more advanced jazz skills. The LISTENING GAMES however could also be of general interest to teachers of other instruments, and some of these games are reproduced briefly below.

I got rhythm

The first player plays a short rhythm on one note and the second player (or group) repeats it. If you play in a group, each player in turn can make up a new rhythm while the others listen and repeat it.

Question and answer

The first player plays a short rhythm on one note and the second player answers with a different rhythm. In a group lesson, simply play in turn.

Action replay

The first player plays a short tune on, say, three notes and the second player or group repeats it. In a group, each player in turn can make a new tune while the others listen and repeat it.

Hands off

The first player makes up a short tune using three or four notes and the next player has to answer it with a different tune. In a group, each player in turn can make up a new tune.

First player → Second player (or group)

Profiling:

In order that the diverse aspects of each pupil's musical development can be organised into a 'structured whole', an example Assessment Profile is printed below.

Half-termly Profile

YEAR: _____   TERM: _____

NAME: _____   CLASS: _____

INSTRUMENT: _____

ASSESS THE STUDENT'S ABILITY TO:—

	Manages extremely well	Manages fairly well	Experiences some difficulty	Experiences much difficulty
Listen sensitively and critically:				
Read music:				
Acquire new techniques on the instrument:				
Interpret music imaginatively:				
Play 'by ear' (Listening Games etc.):				
Improvise:				
Express ideas, emotions (etc.) through composing:				
Notate sounds accurately:				
Contribute positively to group music sessions (Band etc.):				
Show originality in ideas for composition/improvisation:				
Take the initiative over new repertoire:				

Ensemble Scores

The scores provide a general guide to the TEAM WOODWIND ensemble material. However some instrumental combinations include parts which, for musical or technical reasons, will be found to differ occasionally from those printed below.

Flute/Oboe Descant

German Tune

Traditional

Pupil's page 14

Flute/Oboe Descant

Lullaby

Pupil's page 14

Canzonetta

Pupil's page 15

Flute/Oboe Descant

Fast

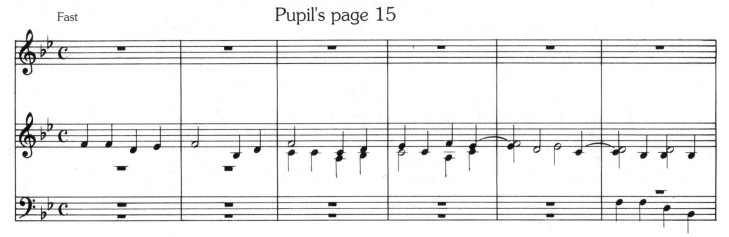

Regal fanfare
Pupil's page 20

Flute/Oboe Descant

Maestoso

When I first came to this land
Pupil's page 20

Flute/Oboe Descant

Fast and furious

Traditional

Blowin' in the wind

Flute/Oboe Descant

Steadily

Pupil's page 21

Words and Music by
BOB DYLAN

Au claire de la lune

Pupil's page 37

Traditional

Little donkey

Pupil's page 37

Words and Music by
ERIC BOSWELL

Tijuana brass
Pupil's page 39

Brightly

I saw three ships
Traditional

Happily
Pupil's page 39

Michael row the boat ashore
Traditional

Moderately
Pupil's page 48

Canzona

ADRIANO BANCHIERI
(1568 - 1634)

Pupil's page 48

O Little Town of Bethlehem

Moderato

Pupil's page 49

Traditional

St. Anthony chorale

Moderato

Pupil's page 49

JOSEPH HAYDN
(1732 - 1809)

March

Pupil's page 55

GEORGE FRIDERIC HANDEL
(1685 - 1759)

Piano Accompaniments

Contents

TITLE	Flute	Oboe
Acapulco Bay	20	20
Auld Lang Syne	25	25
Les Ballons	28	28
Berceuse	33	-
Caribbean Dance	38	38
Elegy	41	41
Menuet Alternat	-	-
Mood Indigo	-	-
Morning has Broken	46	47
Over the Rainbow	50	50
Rigaudon	57	57
Sicilienne	60	60
Sleigh Ride	66	66
Sonata in F	93	-
Sort 'em Out	74	74
Spiritoso e Staccato	-	-
Star Wars	80	80
Stranger on the Shore	-	-
Two Arias	-	90
What a Wonderful World	-	-
When Johnny comes Marching Home	100	100

Bb Clarinet	C Clarinet	Bassoon	Eb Sax	Bb Sax
22	21	20	23	24
25	26	25	27	25
30	29	28	31	32
-	-	-	-	-
38	39	38	40	38
42	42	42	42	43
-	-	56	-	-
-	-	-	44	45
47	46	47	48	49
50	52	50	54	50
57	58	57	59	57
-	-	-	-	-
68	72	72	68	70
-	-	-	-	-
75	76	76	75	77
-	-	78	-	-
80	82	80	84	80
88	86	-	-	-
-	-	-	-	-
-	-	-	96	98
100	101	100	102	100

Acapulco Bay

Flute, Oboe, Bassoon

Acapulco Bay

C Clarinet

Acapulco Bay

Bb Clarinet

Acapulco Bay

Eb Saxophone

Acapulco Bay

Bb Saxophone

Auld Lang Syne

Flute, Oboe, B♭ Clarinet / Saxophone / Bassoon

Auld Lang Syne

C Clarinet

Auld Lang Syne

Eb Saxophone

Les Ballons

Flute, Oboe, Bassoon

Les Ballons

C Clarinet

Les Ballons

B♭ Clarinet

Gently and dreamily

Les Ballons

E♭ Saxophone

Les Ballons

Bb Saxophone

Berceuse

Flute

Caribbean Dance

Flute, Oboe, Bb Clarinet / Saxophone, Bassoon

Caribbean Dance

C Clarinet

Caribbean Dance

Eb Saxophone

Elegy

Flute, Oboe

Elegy
C Clarinet, Bassoon

Elegy
B♭ Clarinet, E♭ Saxophone

Elegy

Bb Saxophone

Mood Indigo

E♭ Saxophone

Mood Indigo

Bb Saxophone

Morning has Broken

C Clarinet, Flute

Morning has Broken

Oboe, Bb Clarinet, Bassoon

Morning has Broken

E♭ Saxophone

Morning has Broken

B♭ Saxophone

Over the Rainbow

Flute, Oboe, B♭ Clarinet / Saxophone, Bassoon

Over the Rainbow

C Clarinet

Over the Rainbow

Eb Saxophone

Menuet Alternat

(Two Galliards) Bassoon

Rigaudon

Flute, Oboe, B♭ Clarinet / Saxophone, Bassoon

Rigaudon

C Clarinet

Rigaudon

Eb Saxophone

Sicilienne

Flute, Oboe

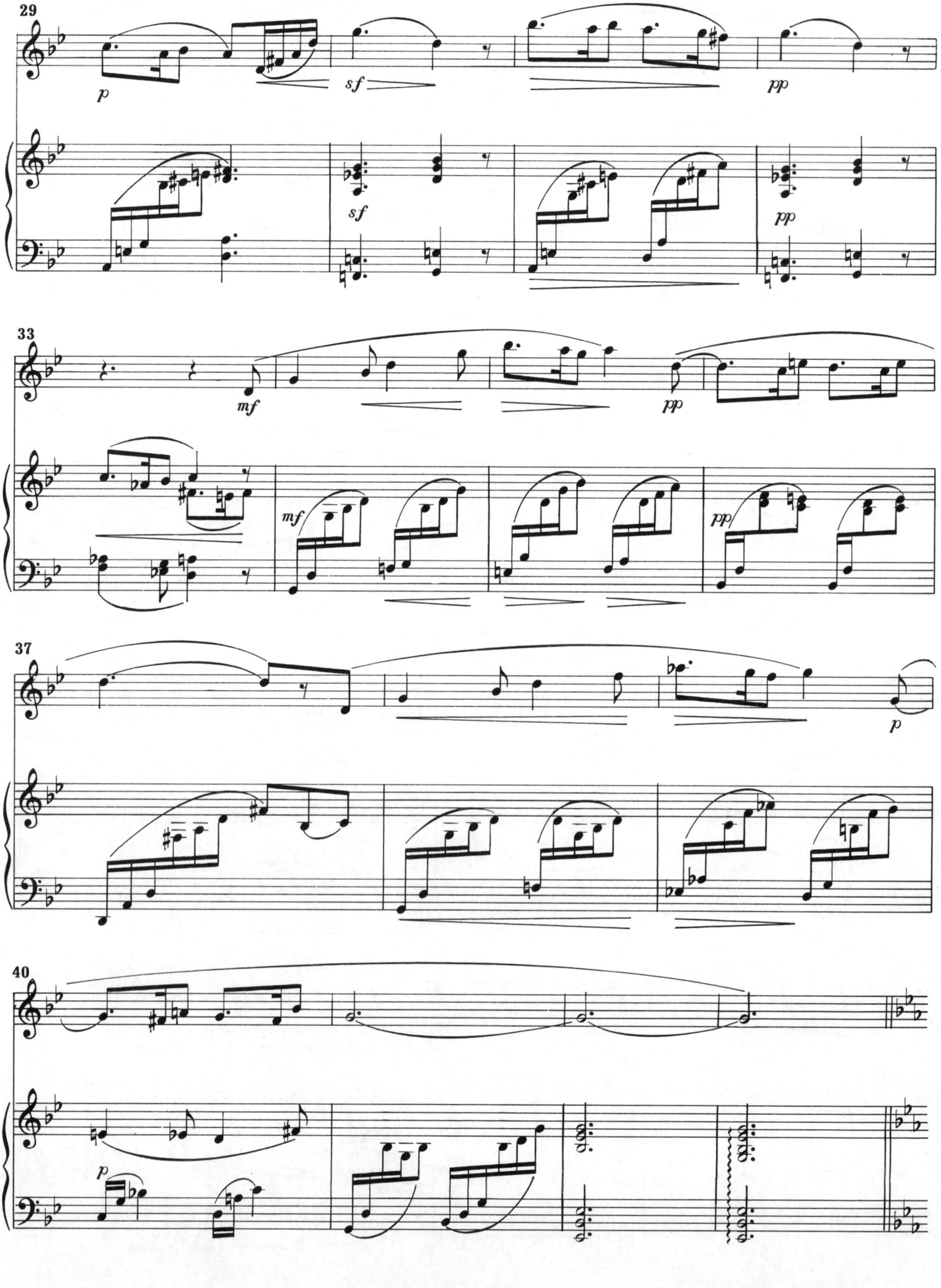
29
p
sf
sf
pp
pp
33
mf
pp
mf
pp
37
p
40
p

Sleigh Ride

Flute, Oboe

very loud

ff

Sleigh Ride

Bb Clarinet, Eb Saxophone

Sleigh Ride

Bb Saxophone

very loud

ff

Sleigh Ride

C Clarinet, Bassoon

Sort 'em Out

Flute, Oboe

Sort 'em Out

Bb Clarinet, Eb Saxophone.

Sort 'em Out

C Clarinet, Bassoon

Sort 'em Out

Bb Saxophone

Spiritoso e Staccato

Bassoon

Star Wars

Flute, Oboe, Bb Clarinet / Saxophone, Bassoon

Star Wars

C Clarinet

Star Wars

Eb Saxophone

Stranger on the Shore

C Clarinet

Stranger on the Shore

Bb Clarinet

Two Arias

Oboe

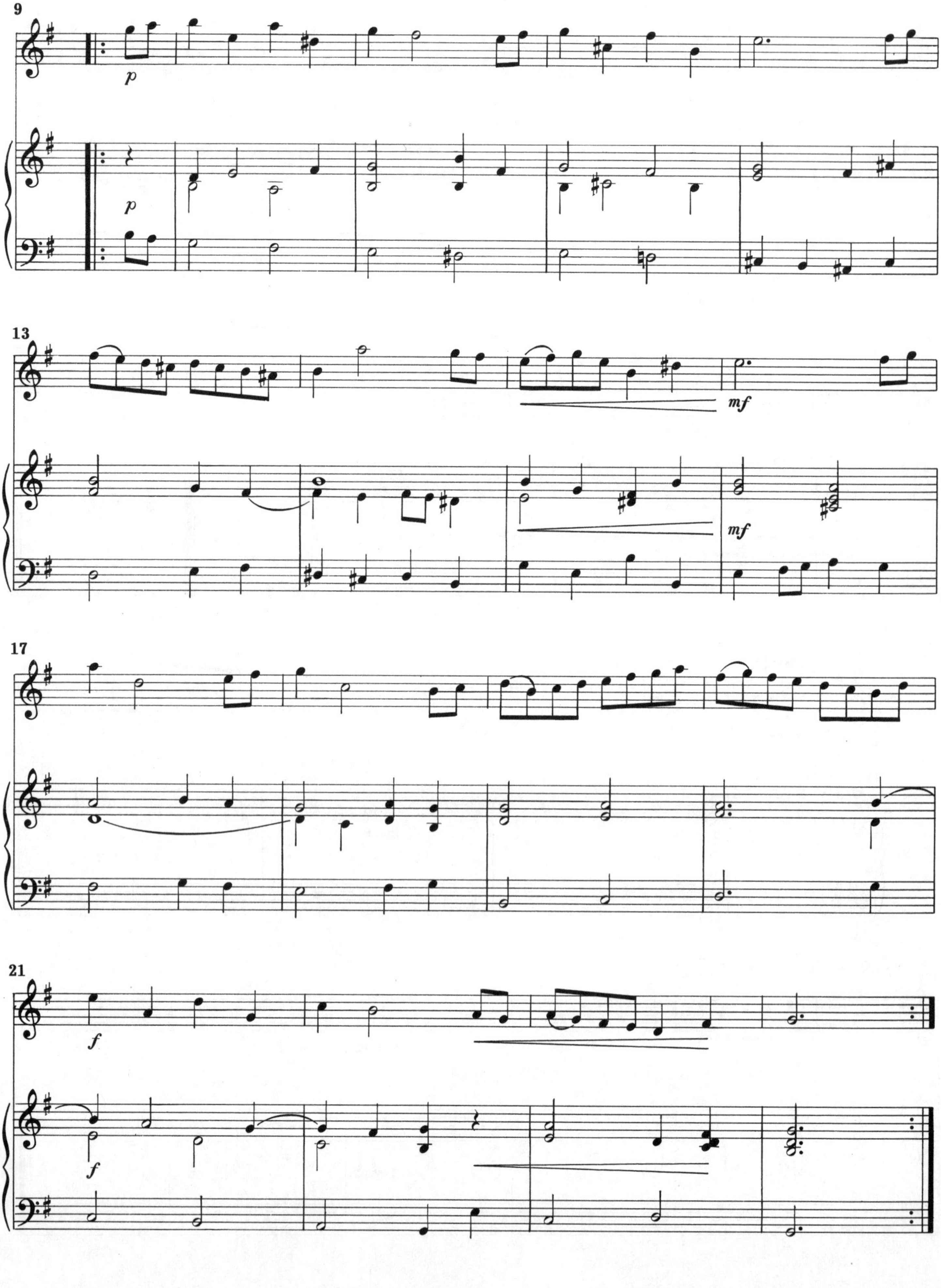
9
p
p
13
mf
mf
17
21
f
f

Sonata in F

Flute

What a Wonderful World

Eb Saxophone

What a Wonderful World

Bb Saxophone

When Johnny Comes Marching Home

Flute, Oboe, Bb Clarinet / Saxophone, Bassoon

When Johnny Comes Marching Home

C Clarinet

When Johnny Comes Marching Home

E♭ Saxophone